Slow Cooking
With
Ms Rose

ISBN-13: 978-1984165282

ISBN-10: 1984165283

Introduction & Dedecation

Slow Cooking

Crock pots, slow cookers, roasters, etc...

Some of the best meals are slow cooked over night or all day. On a hectic day full of work and errands these meals greet you with an awesome aroma when you enter the house.

Join Ms Rose as she shares with you some of her favorite slow cook recipes.

Always remember to share a meal and be a blessing to someone.

Dedication:

This book is dedicated to the ladies of the Gleaners Sunday School class at Vivian First Baptist Church (Vivian, LA). True women of God. They keep it real, lay it on the line, and tell it like it is. They have been there, done that, been to it, came through it, and living witnesses.

Table of Content

Meats
Soups / Stews

MEATS

Brisket

Ingredients
3 pounds beef brisket, fat trimmed
2 teaspoons dried thyme
2 teaspoons himalayan pink salt
2 teaspoons black pepper
1/2 cup chopped onion
2 chopped garlic cloves
1/2 teaspoon cayenne pepper
1 1/2 cups barbecue sauce
1 tablespoons Worcestershire sauce

1) Place brisket in slow cooker
2) In a small bowl combine all other ingredients
3) Cover the brisket with the sauce
4) Place top on slow cooker and
5) Put on low heat for 8 hours
6) Enjoy

Cornish Hens

Ingredients
2 Cornish Hens (Thawed)
2 large red potatoes (cut to 1/2 inch slices)
2 tablespoon of vegetable oil
1/2 teaspoons of garlic powder
1 teaspoons of black pepper
1/2 cup red wine
2 teaspoons parsley

1) Layer potatoes on the bottom of the slow cooker
2) Pour red wine onto potatoes
3) Sprinkle 1 teaspoon parsley on potatoes
4) Mix black pepper, garlic powder, and the rest of the parsley with the oil
5) Rub Mixture onto hens
6) Place hens on top of potatoes
7) Put top on slow cooker
8) Cook on low for 5 hours

Turkey Roast

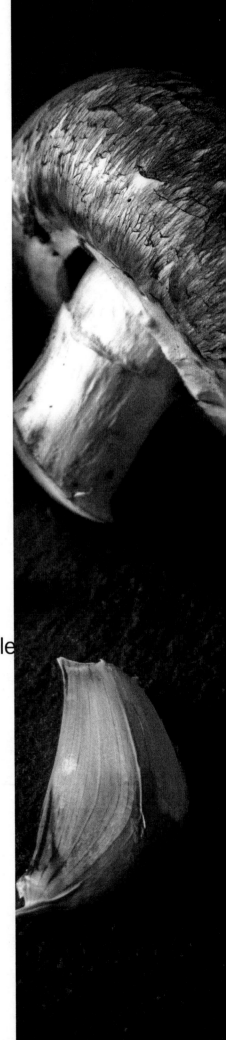

Ingredients

1 (7-9 pound) boneless turkey breast

1/2 cup water

1 cup diced onion

6 whole mushrooms

2 Tablespoons garlic powder

1 Tablespoon onion powder

1 Tablespoon dried parsley

1 Tablespoon Himalayan salt

1 Tablespoon dried oregano

1) Pour water into slow cooker

2) Place turkey, whole mushrooms, and diced onions inside slow cooker.

3) Mix together remaining ingredients and sprinkle over the turkey breast.

4) Cook on low for 8 hours (meat thermometer should read 165 degrees F or greater)

Pork Tenderloin

Ingredients
2-3 lb Pork Tenderloin
1/2 cup Olive Oil
1/2 cup Honey
4 tablesapoons Steak Seasoning
1/2 teaspoon Garlic Powder
1/8 teaspoon Red Pepper Flakes

1) Place the pork tenderloin in slow cooker
2) In a small bowl combine the rest of the ingredients and mix.
3) Pour mixture over the pork tenderloin. Cook on low for 6 hours.

Pulled Pork

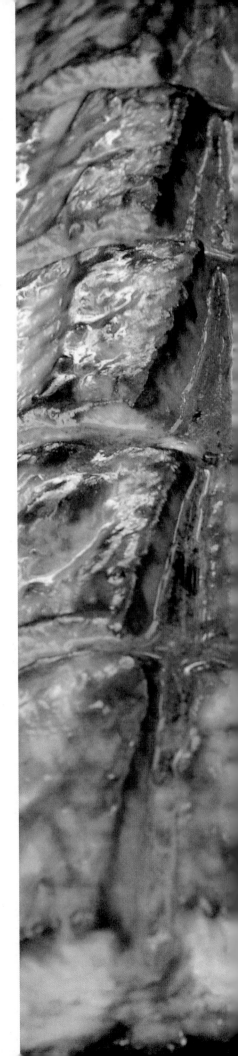

Ingredients

4 pounds boneless pork riblets

2 cups of your favorite BBQ Sauce

1/2 cup brown sugar (optional)

1) Pour 1 cup of barbecue sauce into the slow cooker

2) Add all the riblets.

3) Pour the remaining barbecue sauce over the riblets.

4) Add brown sugar if using.

5) Mix to cover the pork.

6) Cook on high for 4 hours

Bourbon Meatballs

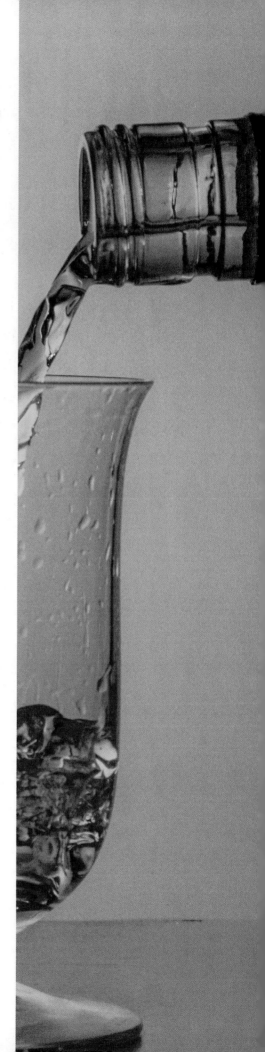

Ingredients
3 lbs frozen meatballs (1/2 oz size)
1 1/2 cup ketchup
1 1/2 cup brown sugar
3/4 cup bourbon or whiskey
3 tsp lemon juice

1) Place meatballs in slow cooker
2) Mix all other ingredients together in a bowl
3) Pour mixture over the meatballs
Pour 1 cup of barbecue sauce into the slow cooker
4) Place top on slow cooker
5) Cook on high for 4 hours

Curry Chicken

Ingredients
3 pounds boneless skinless chicken breast cut in
1 teaspoons salt
12 ounces coconut milk
1 teaspoon curry powder
2 tablespoons cornstarch
2 tablespoons cold water
2 tablespoons lime juice
1/2 teaspoon ground turmeric
1/2 teaspoon cayenne pepper
3 green onions, chopped

1) Place Chicken in slow cooker
2) Mix all other ingredients together in a bowl
3) Pour mixture over the chicken
4) Place top on slow cooker
5) Cook on high for 4 hours
6) Serve with rice

Stews & Soups

My Son's Chili

INGREDIENTS
1 pound ground beef
1 pound smoked sausage in 1/2 inch slices
2 cans black beans
1 can chili beans
1 pound cherry tomatoes
1 medium onion chopped
2 large bell peppers cut in strips
2 jalapeno peppers cut into 1/8 inch slices
1/2 teaspoon Himalayan salt
2 teaspoons chili powder
1 teaspoon cayenne pepper
5 drops of ghost pepper sauce

1) Place ground beef in slow cooker
2) Pour both cans black beans into slow cooker
3) Place sausage in slow cooker
4) Place onions, bell peppers, and jalapenos in slow cooker
5) Sprinkle chili powder, Himalayan salt, and cayenne pepper into vegetables
6) Pour can of chili beans into slow cooker
7) Place cherry tomatoes on top
8) Add the 5 drops of ghost pepper sauce
9) Place top on slow cooker
10) Cook on low for 6 hours

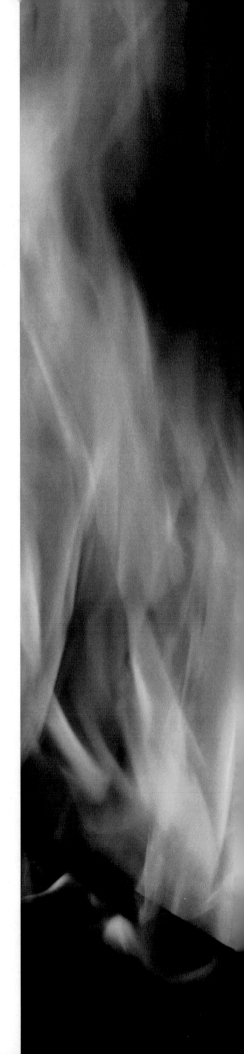

Chicken Pot Pie Soup

INGREDIENTS

2 large boneless skinless chicken breasts
1 cup peas
1 cup yellow corn
1 cup chopped carrots
1 stalk celery, chopped
2 medium potatoes, peeled and diced
1 small yellow, diced
4 ounces cream cheese, at room temperature
4 cups chicken broth
2 teaspoons garlic powder
3 cups heavy cream

1) In slow cooker combine top ten ingredients
2) Place top on slow cooker
3) Cook on low for 5 hours.
4) 25 minutes before serving shred chicken with two forks and stir in heavy cream

Black Bean Soup

INGREDIENTS
2 cans black beans
1 onions diced
1 red bell pepper diced
4 cups vegetable broth
4 garlic cloves diced
2 teaspoons cumin optional
1/2 teaspoon salt
1/2 teaspoon pepper
1 cup corn
1 teaspoon olive oil

1) Place all ingredients into slow cooker
2) Place top on slow cooker
3) Cook on low for 6 hours

Hearty Vegetable Soup

INGREDIENTS
1 pound baby carrot
1 pound potatoes cubed
5 stalks celery sliced
1 can corn
1 can peas
1/2 small onions diced
1 red bell pepper diced
1 teaspoon olive oil
1 tablespoon fresh or dried parsley
1/2 teaspoon dried oregano
1 clove of garlic, diced

1) Place all ingredients into slow cooker
2) Place top on slow cooker
3) Cook on low for 6 hours

Sweet Corn Cilantro Soup

INGREDIENTS

2 tablespoons olive oil

1 teaspoon chili powder

1/4 teaspoon red pepper flakes

1 teaspoon cumin

1 onion, chopped

3 cloves garlic, chopped

4 cups corn kernels

1 small red bell pepper, diced

2 roma tomatoes, chopped

2 cups unsweetened almond milk

1/2 teaspoon

2 ounces of 1 lime

1 teaspoon black pepper

1 tablespoon maple syrup

1/2 cup water

1 cup cilantro leaves

1) Place all ingredients into slow cooker

2) Place top on slow cooker

3) Cook on low for 6 hours

Loaded Baked Potato Soup

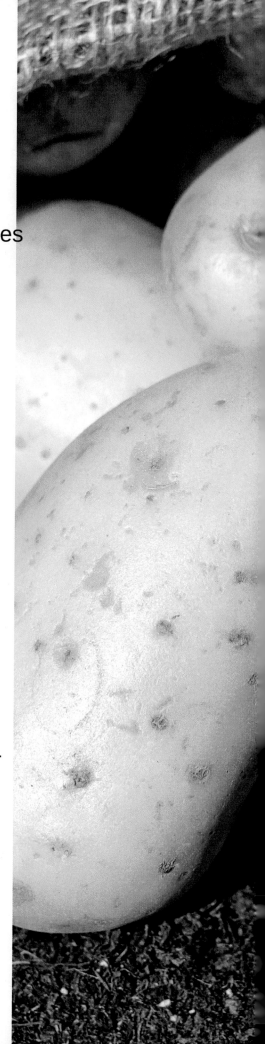

INGREDIENTS

7 medium potatoes, peeled, cut in 1/2 -inch cubes

1 large onion, chopped

2 cups water

3 garlic cloves, minced (or pressed)

1⁄4 cup butter

2 teaspoons salt

2 teaspoons pepper

3 cups heavy cream or half-and-half cream

1 1/2cup shredded sharp cheddar cheese

4 tablespoons chopped fresh chives

1 cup sour cream

10 slices bacon, fried & crumbled

1) Combine first seven ingredients in a large crock pot

2) Add 1 cup of heavy cream to slow cooker

3) Place top on slow cooker and cook on high for 4 hours

4) Mash mixture until soup is slightly thickened.

5) Stir in remainder of heavy cream, 1 cup shredded cheese and chives.

6) In bowl top with sour cream, bacon, and remaining shredded cheese

CookingWithMsRose.com

NOTES

Made in the USA
Columbia, SC
19 August 2022

65693364R00018